# AMAZING

## Brooke Berman

**BROADWAY PLAY PUBLISHING INC**
New York
www.broadwayplaypublishing.com
info@broadwayplaypublishing.com

Cover photo by Brooke Berman
I S B N: 978-0-88145-659-2

First printing: June 2016

Book design: Marie Donovan
Page make-up: Adobe Indesign
Typeface: Palatino
Printed and bound in the U S A

AMAZING was originally commissioned by Childrens Theatre Company (C T C) in Minneapolis through the New Dramatists/C T C Playground initiative. The play was workshopped at C T C, 2003, directed by Melissa Kievman and at New Dramatists, later that year, directed by Ethan McSweeney with consulting and video design by Christine Jones. The play was subsequently developed at CATC in Shepardstown, West Virginia with director Brian Roff and performed at Cypress College in Cypress, CA, with director Mark Majarian.

# CHARACTERS & SETTING

NICKY, *19, a girl who has not yet grown into her own skin. A seeker with a bad home life.*

ISOBEL, *19, also called Is. An "It Girl." Confident. Popular. Sexually active.*

REXX, *19-21, a boy with angel wings and a tambourine. Queer.*

TIGER, *20,* ISOBEL's *ex-boyfriend and a key member of* ISOBEL *and* NICKY's *high school crew. He is recently back from rehab. An instigator.*

*Time: This is primarily a memory play. It takes place in the present with* NICKY *flashing back to the early 2000s, the summer she was 19.*

*Place: Chicago's north side*

For Jamie and Anastasia. With love.

*(2007)*

## How It Began

*(Lights up on* NICKY *in present day, telling her story.)*

NICKY: Both our moms were named Carla.
And both our moms' moms, were named Olivia.
Clearly we were meant for each other.

*(*NICKY *flips a switch, sending us back into the past. The early 00s in Chicago.)*

*(Lights up on* ISOBEL, *19, talking on a cell phone.)*

ISOBEL: It's me, Is. Get here. *(She surveys her surroundings.)* Because you're not going to believe this place.

*(The Piet Mondrian: A weird sterile townhouse on the edge of the cool part of town.)*

ISOBEL: She's gone all summer.

Left me this place. I just got home from school, just got back, and she's like "See ya, Kid. Behave". Hands me keys. Introduces me to her boyfriend! "Fred". Hands me keys. It's—BEHAVE!? Shut the fuck up. It's— *(She makes some gesture to indicate the vastness of this urban art piece called Fred's House and her judgment on it.)*

NICKY: Amazing.

ISOBEL: I think it's cold.

NICKY: Your mom? Or the townhouse?

ISOBEL: He has too much money.

NICKY: Fred.

ISOBEL: My real dad had taste. Never money. But taste. He could fix old stuff and make it look great. His old stuff always looked great.

NICKY: My mom goes for new stuff like Fred. Clean and light. Easily assembled. Colorful. Her husband has no taste. He doesn't like anything.

ISOBEL: How are they?

NICKY: Fighting. They keep threatening to get divorced but you know they won't. Who would they fight with? How do people get like that?

ISOBEL: Sad?

NICKY: Hateful.

ISOBEL: They stop listening. They stop being real. They blame.

NICKY: They like to blame.

ISOBEL: They need someone to blame.

NICKY: Lets not be like that. Ever. Let's *never* be like that.

ISOBEL: We won't. We're different.

NICKY: Promise?

ISOBEL: Sure.

NICKY: The house is kind of great.

ISOBEL: It's free.

NICKY: It's huge.

ISOBEL: It'll help me get to Italy.

NICKY: Italy?

ISOBEL: My new passion.

NICKY: Oh.

ISOBEL: Exactly. So Fred's house is great. For saving money. I'm gonna waitress all summer, put everything away and leave second semester. I can get credit too. The college won't care. Six months traveling: Venice, Florence, Rome, and Tuscany. All those places people talk about.

NICKY: Do you speak Italian?

ISOBEL: I'll learn. How about you?

NICKY: *(Babbling a little, off topic)* Italy? No, I'm more France. I rocked A P French in high school, and I have an intense connection to the French for some reason, I don't know why, but—

ISOBEL: How about you *school*?

NICKY: Oh. That.

ISOBEL: How was it? You didn't say much. In your letters. You sounded—

NICKY: Nicky didn't like school.

ISOBEL: Oh. That's too bad. Is it cuz you stayed local?

NICKY: I don't think so. I mean, I didn't live at home or anything.

ISOBEL: Hm.

NICKY: I think it's me.

ISOBEL: You how?

NICKY: Just me. Nicky doesn't think she belongs anywhere.

ISOBEL: Stop talking about yourself in the third person. It's pretentious.

NICKY: I'm a mutant. My people have no holdings here.

ISOBEL: That's dumb. If you're a mutant, so am I.

NICKY: You're prettier.

ISOBEL: Shut up.

NICKY: Okay. But you are.

ISOBEL: You belong here.

NICKY: Here how?

ISOBEL: Want to stay?

NICKY: Stay how?

ISOBEL: With me. Here. All summer. I mean, if you want. Carla and Fred are gone. They won't care. You could like, live here and help water the plants. I really need help watering the plants *(Gesturing to show that there are no plants)* Come on. Say yes.

NICKY: Yes.

ISOBEL: I couldn't. It makes sense. We won't have to tell each other things anymore—like "this happened" or "that happened" because we'll be living together. We'll *merge.*

NICKY: That sounds uncomfortable.

ISOBEL: Resources. Experiences. Talents. Merge it all. Carla and Fred won't know if you're here, I mean.

NICKY: Well, *my* Carla—

ISOBEL: Right. Overprotective. Tell her it's closer to work. We're gonna have a blast.

NICKY: I don't know. My mom's whole deal is *no.* Always no. Sometimes "absolutely not" —but mostly just no.

ISOBEL: That's dumb because if you were gone she could fight with that guy all the time and not worry.

NICKY: She does that anyway.

ISOBEL: Make it about her. Like, you're doing this to give her space?

NICKY: She won't buy that.

ISOBEL: I want you to stay.

NICKY: You do?

*(This is meaningful.)*

ISOBEL: Hey, look what I found upstairs… *(She reveals a small video camera)* You think my mom and Fred use it to make their own porn?

NICKY: EWWW.

*(ISOBEL laughs.)*

ISOBEL: I'm just kidding. But it's ours now. For the summer. We can shoot stuff. Whatever we want. Collect it and—

NICKY: Let's not edit until the summer's over.

ISOBEL: Good idea. Very Dogma. We'll watch the whole thing in one sitting at the end.

NICKY: We'll have a record. Of our summer.

ISOBEL: Exactly.

NICKY: Unexpurgated.

ISOBEL: Whatever. We'll be—

NICKY: Collecting. Preserving. Capturing.

*(ISOBEL and NICKY explore the camera, holding it, taking it apart, they practice using it—ISOBEL holds the camera on NICKY.)*

ISOBEL: So stay. Can you stay? I want you to stay.

NICKY: Yes.

ISOBEL: Tell the camera.

*(NICKY looks into the camera and smiles. Her image stays silent, embarrassed and fidgeting or else very still, not knowing what to say.)*

*(Meanwhile, the real NICKY turns to the audience and spills her guts.)*

NICKY: The thing is, it's like this. My mom, who has the same name as yours, she's home with her husband, that guy who isn't my dad, and they don't get along too well, and neither one of them gets along with me, and it's better if I'm not there at all because things move there, things move and break—our dishes, glassware, furniture and bodies—things have a way of finding themselves on the other side of the room. They get thrown and they fly, and I get in the way. I don't have any bruises to prove how I get in the way, but I do—get in the way. The dishes hit the wall, and I get called names— "selfish bitch" and "stupid little slut" —which is wildly funny since I'm an eighteen year old virgin with kickass S A T scores and nothing like a stupid slut, whatever he thinks that means. But it's better than what he calls my mom. And what she calls him back. Because let's note that my mom is not a victim of this name-calling garbage, she's a full-on participant. It is a mutual game of torture. Search and destroy. Carla and That Guy search, and they destroy. Each other. And then me. So I love the idea of not going home. I totally love it. Hugely. Deeply. I'm all over it. Yes. I can stay. *(And back in the video as before)* Yes.

ISOBEL: Good.


## Moving In

*(NICKY moves in. She doesn't have a lot of stuff. One big bag full of clothes, a few books, maybe a deck of Tarot.)*

*(The girls spread everything across the floor, trashing Fred's previously pristine house. This is active, physical and fun.)*

*(NICKY turns to the audience:)*

NICKY: We make it ours. Our Space. Our Room. Our House. We trash it. We girlify it. We spread our things all over. My mom has always been extreme when it comes to putting things away. But this summer, I'm not putting anything way. And then, there's the bed. I'm an only child. I've never shared a room with anyone, let alone a bed.

ISOBEL: *(As if interviewing a star on T V)* And how do you feel about that? The bed thing? You feel okay?

NICKY: Yeah. Fine.

ISOBEL: *(Teasing)* No funny stuff.

NICKY: No funny stuff.

ISOBEL: Good. Cause I'd hate to think you were just using me for sex. *(And then, getting another scathingly brilliant idea)* Hey, you know what? Drag the futon out on the deck. Seriously. Look. I think this could be great. We can sleep out here.

*(ISOBEL and NICKY drag the futon outside onto the roof deck—a flat surface that juts out of the upper floor of the house.)*

*(NICKY twirls.)*

NICKY: Amazing.

ISOBEL: Right under the stars.

NICKY: Every night.

ISOBEL: Exactly.

*(ISOBEL and NICKY, once they set up their living space on the roof, throw clothing all over the place, up in the air, on the ground—for NICKY, this is magical. The paper lantern of Streetcar. Enchantment is made.)*

*(ISOBEL starts to look through NICKY's clothes. She finds a great sundress.)*

ISOBEL: Can I wear this?

*(NICKY starts looking through ISOBEL's clothes. Finds something exotic and hot.)*

NICKY: If I can wear this.

(ISOBEL *and* NICKY *exchange smiles and start trying on each other clothes.*)

(*A whole game ensues.* ISOBEL *looks at* NICKY's *body. Really looks at it.*)

ISOBEL: You're afraid to be a woman.

NICKY: What are you talking about?

ISOBEL: That's why you're so weird about sex. It's because you look like a woman.

NICKY: I'm not weird. What are you talking about?
ISOBEL: Nothing.

(*Beat*)

(NICKY *picks up the camera. And changes the subject.*)

(*Later that night, the roof:*)

(NICKY *films* ISOBEL:)

NICKY: Alice Walker says she claimed Zora Neale Hurston as her literary foremother. Who's your literary foremother?

ISOBEL: I don't get the question.

NICKY: Who do you wish your mother was?

ISOBEL: My mother mother?

NICKY: Your art mother. Who do you claim as your art mother?

ISOBEL: Agnes Varda. Mother of the French New Wave. Or Patti Smith. How about you?

NICKY: Anais Nin Her journals were amazing. Full of description and feeling and—history, really. She was lovers with everybody. She wrote erotica for a dollar a page and tons of surrealist fiction, like these stories about how every single thing *feels* all the time, with all sorts of amazing images, like about insect wings—

*diaphanous* this and *ecstatic* that. And she was really
into the early days of psychoanalysis. Jung and Rank.

ISOBEL: That sounds annoying. Patti wasn't annoying.

NICKY: Yeah. Patti. Patti's mine too.

ISOBEL: Because the night! Belongs to Lovers! She wrote
about freedom. Freedom's everything.

*(Beat. NICKY puts the camera down.)*

ISOBEL: I'm glad you're here.

NICKY: You are?

ISOBEL: Totally.

*(NICKY takes the camera into a private area and records
herself. To the camera, as if ISOBEL, her audience, she
confides:)*

NICKY: I take up as little space as possible so that no
one will ask me to leave.
By no one, I mean you.
Sometimes we share a pillow. But mostly I make my
arms into private pillow so I won't have to get too
close. And not because I don't want to. Just because…
I don't know. Just because.


## Tiger Composes An Email

*(Lights up on TIGER, 19, a boy with a lot to say.)*

TIGER: Hola Comprades. Hi there. Hey. Subject
line: Coming Home, Homecoming, not a deliberate
reference to that dance. Heinous custom, that dance.
So yeah. Hola. Hey. Dear Friends at Home. I'm getting
out of here in a few weeks. Coming back. Want to hang
out? I've been thinking about you and I want to hang
out again like we used to when we used to do that. You
know? How we used to get Italian lemonade (cuz I am
not allowed to drink beer and smoke pot), to sit outside

the library and watch people? I'm really sorry about the way I took all of you for granted, used your houses as crash pads when my Dad threw me out, made you hold my stash, passed out, hid out, threw up, all that—and about all those times I just, you know, "stole" if that's what you want to call it. But—hey—Isobel. Dear Isobel, dear razorsedge@hotmail, I've been thinking about the way we used to stay up late and look at the stars and call each other when it rained. Been thinking about that thing you said when we were going out. You said I'd never be lost again. You said I would never be lost because you have an internal compass and I would have you. But I don't have you anymore and I just want to know, were you lying? When you said that? Were you lying? (*He puts the pen down.*) Fuck it. I'll just show up.

### Rules for a New World

ISOBEL: The law of attraction says we create what we focus on. So we need to be clear.

NICKY: Clear how?

ISOBEL: Know what we want. Make a list. And then, achieve everything. It's part of what we're doing here, you and me.

NICKY: At Fred's?

ISOBEL: In our lives.

NICKY: Of course.

ISOBEL: So we need a list. And then, we use the video in a new way. To track the items on the list. And show how we found them. Later when we edit—

NICKY: At the end—

ISOBEL: —we'll edit out the boring stuff.

NICKY: There is no boring stuff.

ISOBEL: There's totally boring stuff. Us with our toothbrushes is boring.

NICKY: What should go on this list?

ISOBEL: Well. First we have to be in the right place.

ISOBEL & NICKY: Café.


## Cafe Express

NICKY: The most sacred place I know. Café Express. I got the job in high school and stayed. Since I go to school locally, I mean, near enough, I mean I don't live at home or anything, but anyhow, what I'm trying to say is—this works out fine. I love it here, it's… like, okay, I'm rambling—will you cut this part later? Right. So, Cafe Express aka "Cafe X", aka "Cafe": small post-hippie Midwestern college bohemians—but Midwestern, so not really dangerous. Not subversive. Get this: John Donne, Nietsche, AND Sonic Youth on the bathroom walls. As grafitti. That's why I love this place. Oh, and some guy has a snake, a real one, a snake. He wears it around his neck. And the skatepunks sit outside on the sidewalk for hours. Cuz one of the things about Cafe Ex is how you can get free refills. SO you spend sixty-five cents on a cup of coffee and you can sit on the sidewalk all day. And everyone smells like patchouli and clove cigarettes and espresso. Which is just fine by me. Just fine. By me.

(*Acid jazz on the stereo.* ISOBEL *and* NICKY *with journals and pens. And the camera*)

ISOBEL: Go back to the list.

NICKY: The list?

ISOBEL: Of stuff

NICKY: Of stuff?

ISOBEL: To find.

NICKY: To find?

ISOBEL: Stop repeating everything I say. The rule is: we have the whole summer to find these things.

NICKY: On the list.

ISOBEL: But we have to find them all.

NICKY: *(Realizing the staff needs her help)* Hold on. I gotta make a latte.

ISOBEL: Make one for me. Daily lattes are part of what we want to create.

*(NICKY goes to make some lattes. REXX passes by ISOBEL. They check one another out, but more like dogs sniffing, less like boy/girl checkout.)*

*(REXX has an earring, a shaved head, a big snake tattoo and angel wings. He also has a tambourine and a harmonica in his bag.)*

ISOBEL: *Hola.*

REXX: *Hola. Como Esta?*

ISOBEL: I don't know. I speak Italian.

REXX: Gotcha. *(He goes back to work.)*

*(NICKY comes back with a latte for ISOBEL.)*

ISOBEL: Who's that? With the wings?

NICKY: New guy. I think his name's Rex. Or Tex. Or Flex. Something like that.

ISOBEL: Hm.

NICKY: So, the list—

ISOBEL: Well. Clearly something with wings.

NICKY: A wing-ed thing. *(She starts writing the items down.)*

ISOBEL: Something Italian. So I can learn about Italy.

NICKY: Authentica Italia.

ISOBEL: Something old—

NICKY: Something new, something borrowed? Like at weddings?

ISOBEL: A marriage. Put a marriage on the list, one that works.

NICKY: I've never seen a marriage that works.

ISOBEL: We'll make one.

NICKY: Okay.

ISOBEL: And we need the signature of a...like an authority person, like a judge...a priest?

NICKY: Separation of church and state.

ISOBEL: How about a cop?

NICKY: Signature of cop.

ISOBEL: And him.

NICKY: Who?

ISOBEL: Angel Wing Boy. He should be on our list.

NICKY: Why?

ISOBEL: I have a really good feeling about him. *(She approaches* REXX *with the camera.)* Want to be in my movie?

REXX: What do I have to do?

ISOBEL: I don't know yet.

REXX: Can I sing?

ISOBEL: *Can* you sing?

REXX: In your movie?

ISOBEL: Oh. I don't know. It's not really a musical.

REXX: It should be a musical. Musicals are coming back in this really major way, they're a totally important form for like, American, art or whatever. *Oklahoma* was a great musical. So was *Dreamgirls*. You should make a movie like the Buffy musical. With a lot of singing that seems to come out of nowhere but then, you know, doesn't. I mean, it doesn't come out of nowhere.

ISOBEL: I was thinking, a documentary about Cafe Express and the people who work here.

REXX: Then I should definitely sing.

ISOBEL: I'm going to Italy second semester.

REXX: Yeah? Why?

ISOBEL: I don't know yet. Tell me about the wings.

REXX: They remind me of flight.

ISOBEL: That's a little like freedom.

REXX: I guess. You know the Joni Mitchell song?

ISOBEL: No.

REXX: It's called Wearing Wings. She's all…do you tape them to your shoulders just to sing? So. I do. Just to sing.

ISOBEL: That's beautiful. Is Joni your literary foremother?

REXX: I don't know. Are you gonna film me or what?

(ISOBEL *pulls turns the camera on and starts to film/interview* REXX. NICKY *joins the pair.*)

ISOBEL: How long have you worked here?

NICKY: And what are your credentials?

REXX: This is my first week here. I like it so far. I used to work at Kava Kave. And before that, I was at Java Jive. I trained at the Big Corporate Place when I lived downstate—but then I took the training and brought it back to the people. I'm kind of like Robin Hood in that way. Once I was in a real restaurant, but it was boring and I was just a runner. You don't make any money as a runner.

(ISOBEL *turns off the camera.*)

ISOBEL: Perfect. I like your tambourine.

REXX: You want to play?

(*Clearly,* ISOBEL *wants to play.*)

ISOBEL: Thank you. I'm Isobel.

NICKY: I'm Nicky.

REXX: I know.

(ISOBEL *plays the tambourine.* REXX *accompanies her with a small harmonica he keeps in his pocket. It is fabulous. An objet trouvee band.* NICKY *joins in with boxes of tea [shaking them] or other percussive found objects. The three are very very good at making music out of these weird things they find. They play until they can't play anymore because they're laughing too hard.*)

REXX: You guys live around here?

ISOBEL: In the Mondrian house around the corner.

REXX: The where?

NICKY: Her mom's boyfriend's place.

ISOBEL: Fred.

NICKY: But we have it to ourselves. My mother's having a divorce and a breakdown so I try to stay out of her way. How about you? Where do you live?

REXX: Andersonville. The House of Boys. Why do you call it the Mondrian house?

NICKY: He's a famous dead artist. And the house looks like his art.

ISOBEL: Sort of. Rectangular. At least.

REXX: Wow.

NICKY: Yes. We know all about Pete Mondrian because of our friend Tiger. He's an artist but he's in rehab but his dad's an artist too and they like this Mondrian person quite a bit.

REXX: He's in rehab?

NICKY: Tiger. Not Mondrian. Mondrian's dead.

ISOBEL: So you want to come over or what?

REXX: I think I do.

ISOBEL: You should. What's your name?

REXX: Rexx. Used to be Robert, but I hate that.

ISOBEL: I'm named after the chick in the Razor's Edge. It's a book.

REXX: Isobel?

ISOBEL: Yeah. but Is is a hottie name, and Iso-bel is not.

NICKY: Nicky isn't really a hottie name. But I'm making do.

REXX: Well, Rexx sure beats Robert. Rex with two xx's Triple X Rexx—

NICKY: That's just double X, actually. Two x's. That's just double, not triple.

REXX: Triple sec Rexx, All night long double X Rexx— how's that?

ISOBEL: I think it's great. My mom's out of town, and she left us in charge of her boyfriend's townhouse. I don't know him too well but he has money.

REXX: Crazy.

ISOBEL: Exactly.

NICKY: We sleep on the roof. We're sisters but we have different moms and dads.

REXX: Yeah?

NICKY: And we're keeping this amazing magic list of all the experiences we need to have to create a good reality.

ISOBEL: So you want to come over or what?

NICKY: But it's only two Xs. You have to choose between 2 x'x or three if you want to be consistent.

REXX: You guys freak me out. In a good way. You freak me out in a good way.

NICKY: Hey is your mom named Carla?

REXX: No. My mom's named Christine.

NICKY: Oh. Well that's okay. At least it's a C.

## Laugh and Sing and Do Your Thing

(REXX *addresses the audience/camera.*)

REXX: They were like, "You want to come over or what?" And I was like, "Yeah". … Hell yeah, I want to come over. I want to come over, come home, jam and play and freak each other out. I want to roll down hills and dance in the street and fucking go to town. Lets go to town. Lets laugh and play in the yard but not too far down the street, not so far that it gets dangerous, but just far enough that it's fun. That's what I want. So yeah, lets go to your place and then keep going on and on and on.

## Why Nicky Can't Go Home

NICKY: Why Nicky Can't Go Home
Nicky doesn't like going home.
Mom says, when are you coming home?
And Nicky says, I say, "I don't know, maybe

tomorrow"
I say, "Staying at Isobel's tonight.
It's late, so I'm just gonna stay".
And I'm here for a few nights—
then a night at Mom's to appease her
and then a week back here.
I never say, no one ever says
I'm LIVING here.
But I am.
But no one ever says it.
And this is how I get to stay.
Don't ask, don't tell.
I don't ask, and no one tells.
Because over there, the air doesn't work.
That place takes the oxygen out of the air
takes the good stuff and leaves only poison.
So there's nothing left to breathe
and the walls start closing in. and the floors rise, and
all the elements reverse. And I know this the way I
know the air is missing the stuff you can breathe.
The stuff that feeds you and not the stuff you run from.
The air over there is all full of the stuff you run from.
The air over here is clean.


## The Dead Person

*(The trio make a video:)*

REXX: Welcome to the Wonder Twins and Me. Special
Episode. Season Opening. The Dead Person.

NICKY: So, first we found Rexx, then we found the
Dead Person. The Dead Person's when our whole
summer really got underway. He wasn't even on our
list.

*(They shift into storytelling mode, getting into a make-
believe car, ready to enact the whole thing:)*

NICKY: We're driving across Webster after buying food at Treasure Island.

ISOBEL: Treasure Island's the food place.

NICKY: We go there cause it's close and Isobel's mom left money for groceries.

REXX: Not for all three of us. I mean, she didn't leave money for all three of us.

ISOBEL: She doesn't even know there are three of us. But she left money for me, and I don't eat too much and it's easy to make it last, to stretch it out—pasta, bread, fruit and lettuce. Who needs much else?

NICKY: Ice cream.

REXX: But we can steal that.

ISOBEL: And we do.

NICKY: We do!?

(ISOBEL *and* REXX *exchange looks.* REXX *changes the subject.*)

REXX: Treasure Island, the food store, has free samples. And a killer soundtrack.

ISOBEL: Elevator music covers of Nirvana. It's disturbing.

REXX: *(Agreeing)* It really kind of is.

(*The three waltz in the aisles of Treasure Island. They dance to elevator music. They eat free samples off all the sample trays. They break this to tell the next part—*)

ISOBEL: So we're driving home when we see him.

*(Kids driving)*

ISOBEL: Stop. That man—Stop—he needs—

(NICKY *stops, as told.* ISOBEL *and* REXX *jump out of the car,* NICKY *follows more cautiously than the other two.*)

(ISOBEL *runs to the old man lying face down in his own backyard, his hands wrapped around a garden hose and water spilling out, and she tries to talk to him, but there is no answer and he is not breathing.*)

ISOBEL: Um... Sir?

(*She stands, looking panicked.* REXX *goes to the screen door behind the house, knocking loudly.*)

REXX: Excuse me... Excuse me... Is anyone here? there's a body...I mean, there's a man...he's kind of...I mean... Could you come look?

NICKY: *(On tape)* So this guy from inside comes out, and he's all "What?" and we're like, there's a guy on your lawn, and he says "Oh, that's Dick. He's just sleeping," And we're like, No. Not sleeping. Dick is not sleeping. And the man follows us to the body and sees that we are right, and he goes back into the house to call the paramedics.

REXX: Isobel goes out into the street and tries to flag cars down. I think she took her shirt off. Did you take your shirt off?

ISOBEL: I was wearing a sports bra. One of those uni-boob things. It wasn't—I mean, I wasn't really taking my shirt off—It's just like, the shirt was red, and—

REXX: Right. She took her shirt off.

ISOBEL: This one guy in a red jeep stops, and says he knows C P R.

NICKY: He thought you were cute.

ISOBEL: No. I think he wanted to help.

NICKY: No. I think he wanted to date you.

REXX: They take turns breathing into the dead guy's mouth.

ISOBEL: Which was wild.

NICKY: And then, pretty soon, all of the dead person's relatives are there, and they're all dressed up. It looks as if they were all at the same brunch or bridal shower just down the road and have arrived in one group. Cousins everywhere. Middle aged women in yellow dresses and school aged children with balloons and uncles with pipes are all standing around the lawn together checking out what's going on. Still no paramedics.

ISOBEL: We did C P R for a long time.

NICKY: Rexx and me, we were back at the car.

REXX: Right. And here's the thing.

NICKY: The thing is, we're having this little problem—

REXX: We can't make eye contact—

NICKY: Because we start laughing.

REXX: Right.

(ISOBEL *rolls her eyes at them—*)

NICKY: And we both know this sucks, we both know it's completely inappropriate—

ISOBEL: Yes. It is.

NICKY: But I look at him, and it's—I know it's awful, I do—but—yeah, it's awful.

REXX: We're going to Hell.

ISOBEL: *(To him)* Well, *you* are.

NICKY: But like, the C P R guy's trying to score points with Isobel, Dick's on the lawn "not sleeping", all those cousins in yellow dresses—and the—did I mention the lawn is covered in these weirdo sculptures? They look like Cracker Jack people.

REXX: I bet Dick made them.

(*Despite herself,* NICKI *snickers.*)

ISOBEL: You're totally going to Hell.

NICKY: Anyway.

REXX: This is when the cop shows up.

ISOBEL: I don't remember this part too well because I was still doing C P R—

REXX: Okay, you weren't really doing C P R. You were like, pretending to do C P R, and that was totally great and well-meaning of you, but you were also completely faking it.

ISOBEL: Hey at least I was doing something!

REXX: Sure. But you don't know shit about C P R.

ISOBEL: I do now.

NICKY: So anyway. The cop comes, and he's like, "Hey what's going on here?" And Isobel and the strange guy with the jeep stop doing C P R, or whatever it is—

ISOBEL: The cop is awful.

REXX: Cops get bored or something and need an activity. Like this guy. Who really needs an activity. In his head he's in an episode of a cop show on T V, he's like—why do they always act like the cops on T V?

ISOBEL: Exactly. So I stand up and say, "I think he had a heart attack,"

NICKY: And the cop goes— (*Laughing too hard to finish*)

ISOBEL: "Has anyone called the paramedics?" And I tell him yes, the guy in the house called the paramedics like fifteen minutes ago, and they're still not here—

REXX: Which is when he gets on "walky". And he's like (*going into his impression of a Super-Butch T V Cop*) ""No paramedics. Okay. Well. Well, you just hold on here. I'll handle it. I'll get it under control. I'll get it together. TEN FOUR TEN FOUR WE HAVE A GENTLEMAN HERE WITHOUT A PULSE—THAT'S RIGHT I SAID

A GENTLEMAN WITHOUT A PULSE. THAT'S
RIGHT OKAY TEN-FOUR.

NICKY: Another moment we really want to laugh.

REXX: No disrespect to the dead, but everyone is in
an episode of "Cops", and it doesn't seem to be doing
much for the guy on the lawn.

NICKY: And Jeep Guy—

ISOBEL: Steve.

REXX: Great.

NICKY: Yeah, him. He keeps trying to flirt with Isobel,
who really just wants to save the dead guy's life and go
home.

REXX: We had groceries to put away. Frozen stuff.
Popsicles.

NICKY: And all of the dead person's relatives, the
cousins, they're getting distracted with the Cracker
Jack sculptures on the lawn.

ISOBEL: So finally the paramedics come, and they hook
him up to a machine. It makes him jump around—

REXX: Marionette puppet, bad string.

ISOBEL: It kind of looks like jump-starting a car. And
then, there's nothing more to do. We can't do anything,
it's just time to go home.

NICKY: So we do. But not before I get the cop's
autograph. For the List. Score one me.

*(They get back into "the car".)*

REXX: Back in car, girls in front, me in back—reverse
shotgun—and we do not say a word. Not a word. We
go up into the house and put the groceries away and
we take our popsicles (red white and blue) up on the
roof with us—

*(Back to "the roof":)*

ISOBEL: And talk.

NICKY: Yeah.

REXX: I think he was a good person.

ISOBEL: Who?

REXX: Dick. The Dead Guy. I can tell he was good.

ISOBEL: You didn't know him.

REXX: No. But I have that sense. That he was good.

*(They eat popsicles.)*

ISOBEL: Do you think we could have saved him?

REXX: No. That was his moment.

NICKY: To die?

REXX: I think people die at the exact right moment.
When they set to the end of their story.

NICKY: I felt like he was watching us.

ISOBEL: I felt that too.

NICKY: We should…do something, right? Say a prayer
or something?

REXX: What kind of prayer? The one for people going
to Hell? Us, not Dick. We're clearly the ones going to—

NICKY: I don't know. I've never prayed before. But
some kind of prayer.

*(They attempt to say a prayer. This is very sincere. They
barely how to know to do it, but whatever it is, it's from their
hearts.)*

ISOBEL: Um, Our Father who left us—I mean who's in
Heaven—Or our Mother—or Someone—

NICKY: Who watches over Children—

REXX: And us. And Dead People.

NICKY: Right. Please watch over Dick.

REXX: Help him transition. To the Dead People side.

NICKY: Help him to cross over in a good way, help all of us find where we belong, help us find home.

ISOBEL: Amen. Popsicle Time.

*(They turn up the music and eat popsicles.)*

ISOBEL: You should live with us.

NICKY: You should.

REXX: Live with you?

ISOBEL: It'll be like a commune. We studied them in this class I took at school.

NICKY: You took a class in communes? Jesus, am I the only person who had to take Math and French and fucking Lit Survey? Your college is just better than mine.

REXX: My mom lives on a commune. Well, it's not a commune exactly, it's a community. They were in a cult and then they left the cult so that they wouldn't be like, mind-controlled, but they stayed living together. They call it a community.

ISOBEL: We'll call ours that too.

NICKY: *(Glee)* Ours. Our own. Yours and mine and yours.

ISOBEL: So, can you?

REXX: Are we gonna find more dead people?

NICKY: Probably not.

ISOBEL: But we'll find something. We have a whole list. We found you.

NICKY: And me. I'm a found thing too, you know.

REXX: I won't live here. But I'll stay over a lot.

ISOBEL: That's okay. That's almost the same thing.

## The Second Dead Person

(ISOBEL *speaks to the camera.*)

ISOBEL: There was one more dead body. A suicide on the train tracks. I didn't find it. He jumped in front of the El. The train's delayed. We're stuck up here. Waiting. (*She turns the camera off.*)

NICKY: Did you see the body?

(ISOBEL *shakes her head, no.*)

ISOBEL: I looked. I wanted to get it on film, but then...

NICKY: Then what?

ISOBEL: It just felt wrong.

NICKY: I understand.

REXX: Well. You know, things happen in threes. I mean, not to be morbid or anything. But things happen in threes.

ISOBEL: What does that mean? A third dead person?

REXX: We should stay alert.

ISOBEL: Alert for another dead person? That's totally stupid, Rexx.

REXX: You never know. Things happen in threes.

NICKY: Dead bodies aren't even on our list.

REXX: I think they are now.

NICKY: Because we found one?

ISOBEL: Two.

REXX: Because they found us.

NICKY: What else will find us?

## Home

(REXX *speaks to the camera.*)

REXX: Home is a good place. I like it at home. I left, but I like it. My mom's downstate. She has eight kids. She lives in that community. My dad lives somewhere else. He wasn't into the whole community thing, I guess. He's pretty straightlaced. So, home's okay, I guess. Couldn't wait to leave, but I guess it's okay. Here, in Chicago, I live with boys. The House of Boys, we call it The House of Boys because only boys live there. I know them from the restaurant. We all worked together at the restaurant. Here was the fun thing about the restaurant—pretending the cappucino maker was broken. "I'm sorry, Sir, you can't have a cappucino; the machine's broken." Big Smile for Tip. Here was the bad thing: uh…everything else.
But I'm gonna have a home someday. Home is the place where you can just be who you are. Where you don't pretend. Where you don't have to be perfect or quiet or take care of anyone you don't want to. Where you can be "at home". Nicky says that sometimes that takes a while to figure out. (*To* ISOBEL, *the camera person*) Interview Over. Time for attack.

(REXX *dives into her, tickling and wrestling* ISOBEL *to the ground. She somehow protects the camera while playing— they dissolve into laughter—*)

ISOBEL: Stop it!

REXX: Stop what?

(REXX *tickles* ISOBEL *hard. She tries to fight him off but to no avail. They look like they're having a blast. Peals of laughter*)

(NICKY *enters, watching them both for a long time before they see her. She does not join in.*)

(*Finally, dissolve*)

## "A is for Annabelle, Grandmother's Doll"

*(A word game)*

NICKY: Acorn.

ISOBEL: Agoraphobia.

NICKY: Asshole.

ISOBEL: Able-bodied.

NICKY: That's a hyphen. Can you use a hyphen?

ISOBEL: Why not?

NICKY: I don't know. It just seems…okay, no, it's okay. Um… A, Apricot?

ISOBEL: Absolute.

NICKY: The adjective or the vodka?

ISOBEL: Adjective.

NICKY: Amphibian.

ISOBEL: Abdominal.

NICKY: Um… A…oh, shit. I can't think of anything. Oh. Anything.

ISOBEL: Doesn't count. That pause was your forfeit. B words. Breathless.

NICKY: Beautiful.

ISOBEL: Barbaric.

NICKY: Barbie doll.

ISOBEL: No proper names.

NICKY: Barbie doll isn't a proper name. If it were a proper name, it'd be Barbie. Barbie doll is the name of the object. It's a brand (B word—BRAND) but not a proper name.

ISOBEL: Okay. You can have Barbie doll. Um…be… bes…bar… Bar. Just bar.

NICKY: Bright.

ISOBEL: Baby.

NICKY: Base.

ISOBEL: Best friend.

NICKY: Me?

(ISOBEL *and* NICKY *exchange a smile.*)

(*Collect from Tiger*)

(TIGER *stands at a pay telephone, an unused cell in his hand.*)

TIGER: Operator? I'd like to place a call.

(*At the Piet Mondrian House*)

(ISOBEL *makes breakfast for everyone. She spreads jam on toast.*)

ISOBEL: He called collect.

NICKY: How'd he sound?

REXX: Who?

ISOBEL: Tiger

REXX: Tiger ?

ISOBEL: Artist. Rehab. Loves us. Always needs bus fare.

NICKY: Used to be Isobel's boyfriend.

REXX: Gotcha.

ISOBEL: In high school.

NICKY: He's—

ISOBEL: Terrible. He's terrible.

NICKY: He's not terrible.

ISOBEL: A mess.

NICKY: Well, you saw that side of him. but he can also be—

ISOBEL: Crazy. Lazy. Needy. "Babe, can I have bus fare? Can I have/can I have?" and sometimes, one gets tired of being the source of someone else's having. Know what I mean? Can I have gets old fast.

NICKY: He had bad parenting.

ISOBEL: So did the rest of us.

NICKY: Yeah. But he really did.

ISOBEL: Whatever. He's a poor little rich boy named after a zoo animal. Whatever.

REXX: So you gonna see him?


## Café Express 2

(NICKY *is behind the counter.* TIGER *appears.*)

TIGER: You still work here.

NICKY: Welcome home.

TIGER: You still work here.

NICKY: You said that. How are you doing?

TIGER: Great. You still—?

NICKY: Want a latte?

TIGER: Sure. Rehab was the best place.

NICKY: Well, that's good.

TIGER: Yeah. It was crazy. We all got really close.

NICKY: Good.

TIGER: And we talked to each other all the time. I made friends. Real friends. Friends who are always there and who are real with each other and don't just take off when things get rough.

NICKY: We're real friends.

TIGER: It's different.

NICKY: How different?

TIGER: Just different. How's your mom? I love your mom.

NICKY: She's okay. Getting divorced.

TIGER: For real?

NICKY: Who knows.

TIGER: That guy she's married to is a jerk.

NICKY: I know.

TIGER: An asshole.

NICKY: I know.

TIGER: So she's good?

NICKY: Why don't you think we're real friends?

TIGER: I didn't say that.

NICKY: You did.

TIGER: Don't get so defensive. Just, you know. Things. How things get.

NICKY: How do things get?

TIGER: I don't know. You tell me.

NICKY: I don't know what you're talking about. And you're starting to bug me.

TIGER: You've been hanging out with Isobel too long.

NICKY: I think things turn out just great. Just the way they're s'posed to.

TIGER: Okay. Sure. You can tell yourself that for a really long time.

NICKY: Uh, you want a latte or not? And you have to pay for it. I got in trouble last time I gave you all that free shit.

TIGER: I have money.

NICKY: Good. Cuz I got in trouble.

TIGER: Wow, you think you know who your friends are….

NICKY: I'm just saying you have to pay for your coffee, that's all. If I get caught, I have to pay for it out of pocket.

TIGER: What are you like, keeping a record?

NICKY: Forget it.

(TIGER *hands* NICKY *a dollar. She looks at it, looks at him, puts it in her pocket. Turns to enter the next scene—*)

## Rehab Was Fun

NICKY: Is rehab supposed to be fun?

ISOBEL: It's Tiger. Who knows.

NICKY: Are you going to see him?

ISOBEL: Why would I do that?

NICKY: Because he's our friend?

ISOBEL: He's your friend. He's not my friend.

NICKY: Will you ever say that about me?

ISOBEL: How should I know? Will you ever do anything that would make me want to say that about you?

NICKY: I don't think so.

ISOBEL: Tiger's bad news. He always was. Have you seen Rexx today? Where is he?

NICKY: Don't know.

ISOBEL: He hasn't called since last night.

NICKY: Something he doesn't.

ISOBEL: He always calls first thing.

NICKY: Maybe he's sleeping.

ISOBEL: Maybe.

NICKY: I was thinking about the list. Defining moments.

ISOBEL: I don't know what you mean.

NICKY: Watersheds. Breakthroughs. Revealations. I think we should add those moments to the list.

ISOBEL: Defining moments.

*(Beat)*

NICKY: What would make you not want to see me?

## Like A Virgin

TIGER: What the fuck's a watershed?

NICKY: It's that moment where you see two paths. Like you climb up on the watershed and you realIsobele something about your life and your choices and you make one, a choice—and then you're like, "Wow. That was really a watershed."

TIGER: Dude, you sound like some Lesbo folk song.

NICKY: Have you had one? That's all I want to know. Have you had a watershed? Didn't you have them all the time in rehab?

TIGER: Are you in love with Isobel?

NICKY: Are you on drugs?

TIGER: Unfortunately no. Not anymore.

NICKY: Sorry.

TIGER: Whatever. Just want to know what's going on there at the Mondrian House.

NICKY: Nothing.

TIGER: You think you're queer?

NICKY: No.

TIGER: Just asking. Don't have to get all defensive. Or do you?

NICKY: Shut up.

TIGER: Oh. Maybe you do…

NICKY: So you haven't had a watershed?

TIGER: Oh I forgot.

NICKY: Forgot what?

TIGER: You're defensive because you're still a virgin.

NICKY: Seriously lay off, Tiger.

TIGER: And really, we don't know what you are yet. I mean, gay or straight. Or whatever the fuck's in between.

NICKY: Shut up.

TIGER: One day I should just lay one on you. Big wet kiss on the mouth. So we can tell for sure.

NICKY: Yeah, maybe. *Not.*

TIGER: Well, think it over. I hate to see you suffer like this.

NICKY: Suffer?

TIGER: Sexual frustration.


## The Roof

NICKY: Tiger's out of control.

ISOBEL: And that's new how?

NICKY: Yeah. I love you guys. I really ldo. I want you to be my family.

ISOBEL: We are your family.

REXX: I hate this show.

NICKY: What show?

REXX: The one we're in right now. Bad reality T V. Confessional teens from bad homes.

ISOBEL: Confessional pregnant teens. From bad homes. That sounds like a band.

NICKY: But I do. Love. This. How we are. Together.

ISOBEL: But do you have to talk about it all the time?

NICKY: You said—

ISOBEL: We create what we focus on. Let's just focus on—

REXX: Focus on me. Focus on me, and the rest of your life will be brilliant.

ISOBEL: Or boring.

REXX: Or best-ever.

ISOBEL: Or "beside the point".

REXX: Focus on me and your life will shine.

NICKY: My life is kinda shining. Right now. That's all I'm trying to say. And I want it to—

REXX: Focus on me!

NICKY: You know.

ISOBEL: To what?

NICKY: Last.

ISOBEL: Nothing lasts. Watch the movie.

*(She does. Then* NICKY *picks up the camera, leading us to:)*

## The Perfect Mocha

*(The three make another video.* ISOBEL *takes the camera from* NICKY.*))*

REXX: Here we are. On a quest.

ISOBEL: Cut.

REXX: What?

ISOBEL: Don't say "quest". Say "search"—

REXX: Quest is better.

ISOBEL: You think?

NICKY: Stronger noun.

ISOBEL: Okay. Say quest.

REXX: Right. So don't stop me again.

ISOBEL: Take Two. Search for the Perfect Mocha.

NICKY: Here we are.

REXX: On a *quest*—

NICKY: For the perfect mocha latte.

REXX: The most inoffensive drink on the planet. They're like iced chocolate milk. But better.

NICKY: True. And we know this because we are both trained iced mocha latte professionals. Really.

REXX: Chicago has a lot of cafe's and coffeehouses. And we're going to visit them all.

(NICKY *holds up an iced latte in a plastic cup.*)

NICKY: This one, Cafe Express. I'd give it a nine, how about you Triple X Rexxx?

REXX: Umm, eight. I'd say eight—mostly because I know the girl who made that one, and it wasn't either one of us, so it's an eight. Lets check out the competition, shall we?

ISOBEL: Java Jive.

REXX: Kava Kave

NICKY: Scenes.

ISOBEL: No Exit

REXX: The Heartland Café. They have live music.

NICKY: The red place. The green place. the place down the road from Oz Park with the good bread.

ISOBEL: I love that bread.

REXX: We can make it at home.

ISOBEL: Not the same thing.

NICKY: The joy of the café is, well, the café. Mocha in a public place.

REXX: I'm bored.

ISOBEL: You can't be bored.

NICKY: One more.

REXX: This is it.

ISOBEL: This *is* it. This is my favorite.

NICKY: My favorite too.

REXX: A ten.

NICKY: Where's it from?

REXX: Guess.

NICKY: I don't know.

REXX: Starbucks.

ISOBEL: Shut up.

REXX: The indies are losing ground.

NICKY: Try another.

ISOBEL: Lets just say Café, and leave it at that.

REXX: But that's a lie.

NICKY: The Search For The Perfect Mocha, take two.

REXX: Oh no oh no oh no—this is *it*. This is it, this is it, this is it…and…

*(The video gets turned off.)*

## You Are Not Even Gone Yet

NICKY: This is the dream I keep having. I come home from school, only I'm coming home to your house. I have a key. But I get there and your mom's home and you're not around and I get the feeling that I am not wanted. Not welcome. So I go. I go across the hall to my apartment, where I live with my own mom. But my mom's gone too and it's all empty over there, my place, and dark, it's all dark, and I open up the blinds to let the light in. I do this. I let the light in because my mom's left it totally dark. And then I notice how my mattress is all ripped us and the stuffing's coming out from inside and it's all ripped open and exposed, springs and weird cords and foam—and the loneliness makes me cold and it won't go away. And that's when I miss you. And I can just do that for hours. Miss you.

*(A Defining Moment)*

REXX: So then she's like, don't tell your father if you think you're a Homo. And I'm like, what do you mean don't tell my father? And what do you mean "if I think"? I don't know yet, I mean, I don't know. Maybe. Destination unknown, Dude. I mean, maybe. I mean, I don't know. But she's very clear on this point. Whatever you do, don't tell your father if you think you might be queer. Because you will be dead to him. Dead. And suddenly I can't look my father in the eye anymore. I don't know, I just can't. I can't look my mom in the eye either. So I leave. I say, I'm going to the City. I save my money and I get on a bus, and I go. I just go…I think that was my defining moment. I mean, I think that was it. Have I had one lately? No. But maybe I'm about to. Do you think we get more than one? I mean, like, in a lifetime?

NICKY: I do. I think we get more than one.

REXX: Well that's good. Cause I'd hate to be done.

## Just Saying Stuff

ISOBEL: It's not that I've never had a "defining moment." Because I have. I'm sure I have. Like with Tiger, probably. I mean, there was a lot to that whole time, that time with him, and it's—it probably defined me. You know. That last week. Before he got caught When he ran away. When we hid together. When he cried. And I saw him cry. And we, you know, we whatever made love. And he got sent away. And I stopped writing. And I saw. What my mom kept saying. About him. And who he was. What he takes. What my mom said, she said, she said—he'd eat me alive. , And she was right. She said we'd kill each other. And that I should move on. Because I'm young. I'll have other chances. To feel loved. Like that. To feel real. To feel—important. That's not love, she said. Feeling important. She said, that's ego. My mom knows a lot about men. She's certainly been with enough of them. So when she says something's not love... (Beat) ...I don't like being on this side of the camera.
Let's switch back.

## Who Are We Supposed to Love?

(ISOBEL and REXX are kissing.)

REXX: Have you said anything?

ISOBEL: No. Do you think I should?

REXX: No.

ISOBEL: Yeah. Me either. I don't think I should either.

REXX: Okay. Well, I won't.

ISOBEL: Me either.

REXX: Okay.

*(Beat)*

ISOBEL: You think it's okay?

REXX: I do.

ISOBEL: Okay.

REXX: So don't worry.

ISOBEL: I won't.

*(ISOBEL and REXX kiss again. Like lovers)*

ISOBEL: There are all sorts of things I don't get.

REXX: Like what?

ISOBEL: All of it. Who we're s'posed to love. And why.

REXX: We're s'posed to love each other.

ISOBEL: How do you know?

REXX: Just do.

ISOBEL: But you're—

REXX: So?

ISOBEL: Yeah. How do you know? If you are, I mean.

REXX: I'm still trying to figure it out, I guess.

ISOBEL: Me too.

REXX: You too what?

ISOBEL: Trying to figure it out.

REXX: Listen, I don't think we should worry too much. Lets just let it happen, okay? Besides, I think you can be queer with complication. Right?

ISOBEL: Do you think Nicky knows?

REXX: That we're kissing?

ISOBEL: Yeah.

REXX: Nicky doesn't know.

ISOBEL: She'd never think about anything like this.

REXX: No. She kind of worships everyone. She sees what she wants.

ISOBEL: Sometimes it bugs me. Makes me want to act bad. Because she thinks I'm so good.

REXX: She's learning. We're all just trying to grow ourselves up. You know?

ISOBEL: But the way she needs me, it kind of freaks me out. What if I let her down?

REXX: Then you let her down. Then what?

ISOBEL: We can't help it sometimes, right? I mean, her expectations are completely— *(She notices the camera is on.)* Oh fuck. Hang on—

*(ISOBEL turns it off as NICKY enters.)*

NICKY: Hey guys.

ISOBEL/REXX: Hey—

REXX: How was work?

NICKY: Jackie Q bugs the shit out of me. And her shots are watery. I always have to remake the espresso.

REXX: She pulls too fast.

NICKY: Yes!

*(The phone rings. ISOBEL goes to answer it. Picks up the receiver.)*

ISOBEL: Buon giorno? *(Beat)* Wrong number.

REXX: That's cuz you answered the phone like a freak. Hello, Fettucine Alfredo?

ISOBEL: You're asking for it.

NICKY: We're a nonviolent household. Come on!

REXX: Hey the thing on the list about marriage? This is one. We cook for each other and fight.

*(The three are in agreement.)*

ISOBEL: One of the better ones I've seen.

NICKY: Way better than my mom's. Except it's unconsummated.

(ISOBEL *and* REXX *share a look.*)

NICKY: What?

ISOBEL/REXX: Nothing.

NICKY: You know I think my defining moment is you. Both of you. This. It's—

(ISOBEL *looks guilty.*)

NICKY: *(Off her look)* What?


## Amazing All the Time

*(At Café Express)*

TIGER: Does everything have to be "amazing" all the time ?

NICKY: Excuse me?

TIGER: Why does it have to be "amazing?" Can't it just, be fine?

NICKY: But it is amazing. This is the best time I've ever had in my entire life. We made this mocha latte video and we met this waitress from Cafe Pergolesi and she's an actress and she knows, like, tons of people, and this girl Helen has a ghost at her house. We found two dead bodies—well, we only found one, but Isobel saw the second one on the El. And we meet people all the time—Thomas from Cafe Express, Helen from Java Jive, the twins at the beach, the old lady who lives on Isobel's street, Rexx's roommates at the House of Boys. It's all pretty amazing.

TIGER: I think you like to see it that way.

NICKY: No. What's the difference?

TIGER: The difference is that you're insecure and you need to tell everyone that your friends are amazing because it's not enough for you to just be real.

NICKY: Okay, slow down. This isn't Rehab. This is my summer.

TIGER: I'm just saying... You might want to go to a meeting with me.

NICKY: You might want to not tell me what to do.

TIGER: The people you like, we're all just people. Isobel? Oh, please. You think she's some kind of goddess?

NICKY: She kind of is.

TIGER: No. That's just your thing. If she's a goddess, then you get to be the goddess's friend, and doesn't that make you special? It's ego.

NICKY: I don't like you anymore.

TIGER: Sure you do. I'm the only one who's real.

NICKY: Okay, that's just silly. And what's "real" anyhow?

(NICKY *is referring to something larger than life about the way* TIGER *dresses—he has a costume of sorts. This is a valid observation on her part.*)

TIGER: I'm just saying, all this "amazing" stuff—it's all you. Projecting around into the void, into empty heartless people who will fuck you up later.

NICKY: No. That's not true. That is not true at all.

TIGER: Someday you will thank me.

NICKY: You're wrong.

(*Beat. Then:*)

NICKY: Remember that thing you said?

TIGER: Was it brilliant?

NICKY: No. But it was bold.

TIGER: I don't know what you mean.

NICKY: I think we should.

TIGER: Should what?

NICKY: Chicken.

TIGER: I have no idea what you're talking about.

NICKY: Yes you do. It was your idea. So I'll know what I am.

(NICKY *boldly kisses* TIGER. *At first, it's surface—she's just trying to freak him out—*)

NICKY: Well, there. I like boys. But I don't like you. *(She's proud of herself for getting him back. She starts to walk away and then—)*

TIGER: Hey, wait.

(TIGER *kisses* NICKY *back. It's more sexual this time, and she kisses back. Now they're both stunned.)*

NICKY: I don't like you at all. *(She leaves.)*

(TIGER *takes out his cell phone and makes a call. Hangs up before anyone answers.)*

*(At the same time:)*

*(The phone rings in the Mondrian House. No one answers.)*

## The Roof

(ISOBEL *and* REXX *lie with their heads on one anothers bellies.* NICKY *is nearby—)*

ISOBEL: I want to have babies. A lot of them. Soon.

REXX: How soon?

ISOBEL: Soon. And I'm going to raise them in a big old loft.

REXX: Count me out. I'm not in that picture. *(Summoning* NICKY*)* Get over here. Your friend wants to breed.

*(*NICKY *joins them, puts her head on them as well.)*

NICKY: Now?

ISOBEL: What's the big deal? We can't stay kids forever.

REXX: Why not?

NICKY: Are you having babies before or after Italy?

ISOBEL: I don't know.

REXX: You could have babies during Italy.

ISOBEL: In Italy. With an Italian. My grandparents would be psyched. If he's Sicilian, even better.

NICKY: I don't want babies. I don't know why. But I don't want them.

REXX: Me either. Unless it was all three of ours and we taught it cool songs to sing. That'd be okay.

NICKY: Yeah. That would be okay. Isobel could have it. I don't need to have it.

ISOBEL: I'll raise my baby with you guys. Go to Italy, get pregnant, come home. Raise baby on roof? Teach it cool songs. Put it in our movie.

*(Her phone rings. Caller Unknown)*

ISOBEL: Studio. Carmen Speaking.

*(A hang-up. She turns to the others.)*

ISOBEL: It's Tiger. Calling and hanging up.

REXX: Are you sure? *(He glances at the phone.)* Unknown caller.

ISOBEL: It's him.

*(The phone rings again.* NICKY *answers this time.)*

NICKY: Tiger stop calling us.

*(A hang up.)*

*(Then the phone rings again.)*

ISOBEL: *(Sweetly)* Hello? *(Beat)* Stop it, stop it, stop it! *(She furiously hangs up the phone.)*

ISOBEL: He has to be stopped.

NICKY: I'll handle it.

ISOBEL: Good. Cuz he's gonna be the third dead body.


## Warped

NICKY: Are you prank calling us?

TIGER: Pray do tell, what does that mean?

NICKY: Prank calling us. Are you calling and hanging up?

TIGER: Why-ever would I do that?

NICKY: Because I'll tell your sponsor if I find out it's you. And Isobel'll beat you up. And she'll probably kill you too, don't think she won't.

TIGER: I'm not "prank-calling" you.

NICKY: Good.

TIGER: You're warped.

NICKY: Someone is calling us and hanging up. Sounds like you, that's all.

TIGER: I have better things to do than prank call a couple of girls.

NICKY: And Rexx.

TIGER: Yeah, like I said.

NICKY: Stop acting like you're better than us.

TIGER: Pot calling kettle black?

NICKY: Fuck you, Tiger.

TIGER: You really want to, huh?

NICKY: Hey, I think kissing you was another defining moment. Defining how you suck.

(REXX *appears.*)

REXX: Okay, Nick At Night. Time to hit road. Relief arrives. In the form of Me. Enter me. Relief. Your shift over. Mine begins. Hours and hours of Sonic mocha. Earl Grey tea and the milk steamer face Triple X Rexx. What will he do? How will he survive? Where will Nick at Night go? All these questions and more would be answered with the camera, only Little Miss Someone had to take it to—where'd she go again? Where did she go? (*Sees* TIGER) Oh. You must be Leopard.

TIGER: Tiger.

REXX: Whatever. Everything okay here?

NICKY: Yeah. It's fine.

(*He goes to put his stuff away—*NICKY *turns to* TIGER.)

NICKY: You coming?

TIGER: I think I'll stay.

NICKY: You can't—

TIGER: Can't I?

NICKY: Well. (*She seems reluctant to leave him alone with* REXX) Well, you remember what I said, okay?

TIGER: Okay.

(REXX *returns as* NICKY *is leaving.*)

NICKY: Roof at ten?

REXX: Totally. Adventures.

(NICKY *leaves.* REXX *turns to* TIGER.)

REXX: Leave her alone.

TIGER: Her?

REXX: You know what I mean.

TIGER: I don't know what you're talking about.

REXX: Isobel. Leave Isobel alone.

TIGER: Who are you? God?

REXX: Sometimes. Sometimes I'm a lot like God.

TIGER: I don't know what you mean.

REXX: I mean that you're stalking Isobel and it's scary and weird so just like, lay off, okay?

TIGER: Okay, first of all, I don't know who you are and I don't acknowledge you, or your right to tell me what to do and when—not to mention who to stalk—or not. Second, you don't know Isobel. You may think you do. But you don't. I'm the only one who really knows her, okay? Go home, Queer Boy.

REXX: Fuck you.

TIGER: No. Fuck you. Fucking faggot.

(REXXx *throws a punch at* TIGER. TIGER *ducks. They sort of fight, but mostly* REXX *is the aggressor and* TIGER *manages to duck or prevent him from doing anything too major. It's more insulting this way.* TIGER *just resists fighting* REXX.)

TIGER: Whoa Dude. I'm a pacifist. Chill out, huh? You flamers can't fight for shit.

(TIGER *takes out his cell phone and leaves.* REXX *is really upset.)*

REXX: You chill out, Asshole.

(TIGER *is now gone.)*

REXX: Goddamn—

(REXX *throws himself into some kind of fight/dance to something like The Cure which morphs into real dance music and now, he is at a club, dancing.)*

*(Berlin)*

REXX: Hey. I'm Jack. What's your name? Come here often? I'm a Leo. How about you? What's this place called again? Berlin? Perfect. I got the right boots for Berlin. Want to keep going? Dance all night long? I can dance all night long. Yeah, my name's Jack. J-A-C-K. Hey, I know this place called Underground Railroad. Two for one drink specials. Gotta wear eyeliner. You into that?

## The Remnants of Eyeliner

*(At Café, the next morning)*

REXX: You don't usually work this shift.

NICKY: Covering for Jackie Q.

REXX: That's cool.

NICKY: You were out last night.

REXX: Yeah.

NICKY: We tried calling.

REXX: I know. I was out.

NICKY: We were going to meet on the roof. Remember?

REXX: Yeah. I guess.

NICKY: Did you have fun?

REXX: Sure.

NICKY: What'd you do?

REXX: You know. Just… Stuff.

NICKY: Like what?

REXX: Just stuff.

NICKY: We tried calling. Left messages.

REXX: I know. I don't have a cell phone, can you believe that we don't have cell phones? We have a video camera, but—

NICKY: Do you still like us?

REXX: Sure I do. I just…needed to go out.

NICKY: Oh.

REXX: With boys. I was out with boys.

NICKY: Oh.

REXX: Just doing stuff. Boy stuff.

NICKY: Guns and porn?

REXX: Gay stuff.

NICKY: Drag and porn?

REXX: Um, no. I'm not exactly a drag type.

NICKY: What type are you?

REXX: I'm trying to figure that out…

NICKY: Yeah?

REXX: Yeah. I have some stuff I have to figure out.

NICKY: Can you figure it out with us?

REXX: No. I can't.

(REXX *walks away,* NICKY'*s left there. Hurt*)


## Figuring Stuff Out

NICKY: What's up with Rexx?

ISOBEL: What do you mean?

NICKY: I don't know. Why can't he figure his stuff out with us?

ISOBEL: I don't know.

NICKY: Do you think he's okay?

ISOBEL: Sure. Of course he's okay.

NICKY: Are you okay?

ISOBEL: Sure.

NICKY: Okay.

ISOBEL: Okay.

NICKY: Is this our first fight?

ISOBEL: We're not fighting.

NICKY: What about us and Rexx? Is it our first fight with Rexx?

ISOBEL: We're not fighting. Rexx is just, you know, he has stuff to do.

NICKY: Oh.

ISOBEL: So we're not fighting. No blame, remember? Everyone takes responsibility for his or her own deal. And no one blames.

NICKY: I know.

ISOBEL: Right. So we're totally fine with Rexx needing a break.

NICKY: Do you need a break?

ISOBEL: No.

NICKY: Good. Because me too. I never need a break from you.

ISOBEL: Good.

NICKY: Tiger thinks I'm in love with you. Isn't that funny?

ISOBEL: You are in love with me. I'm in love with you too. We're all three in love with each other.

NICKY: Does that make us...?

ISOBEL: It doesn't make us anything.

NICKY: Do you ever think about it?

ISOBEL: No.

NICKY: Me either.

ISOBEL: Not with you. I mean, sometimes. But not with you.

NICKY: Oh.

ISOBEL: That's not who we are to each other.

NICKY: Okay.

ISOBEL: Is it okay?

NICKY: Sure. Of course it's okay. Oh my God, it's totally okay. But—you think about it with other girls?

(ISOBEL *says nothing.*)

NICKY: Okay.

ISOBEL: You can't kiss people you love that much. Except Rexx.

NICKY: Except Rexx what?

ISOBEL: Well. I can kiss Rexx.

NICKY: You kiss Rexx?

ISOBEL: I thought you knew.

NICKY: Uh, no. No. I didn't know.

ISOBEL: Oh. I thought you did.

(*Silence*)

ISOBEL: It's on the tape.

NICKY: We don't watch the tape. Remember? We don't watch and we don't edit it. Until summer's over. You said—I mean, I figured we'd have a whole *watching* ceremony. And then editing…

ISOBEL: We never said don't watch. Don't edit. But we never said don't watch.

NICKY: Yes we did.

ISOBEL: No. We didn't.

*(Weird, awkward silence)*

ISOBEL: What?

NICKY: Nothing. It's just—I would kiss you. If I were kissing girls, I'd kiss you. Why wouldn't you kiss me?

ISOBEL: I don't know. We love each other.

NICKY: Isn't that who you're supposed to kiss? The people you love?

ISOBEL: Not like that. I mean, not like that.

NICKY: I don't get it. Why not like that? Who are you supposed to kiss then?

ISOBEL: I don't know. But not the people you love like that.

*(NICKY looks pensive.)*

ISOBEL: What?

NICKY: Well…I'm just wondering…I mean…you know, trying to …

ISOBEL: Just say it.

NICKY: I'm wondering who we're supposed to love. Like that.

ISOBEL: I don't know. Honestly. I wish I did.


## Watching a Famous Trilogy

*(ISOBEL, NICKY and REXX. All together. Eating popcorn and watching a movie.)*

REXX: Can we watch the first one? The first one is so much better.

ISOBEL: No, I like this one. And then we have Italian movies. A whole bunch of Fellini. For research.

REXX: Okay, you're not going to Italy.

ISOBEL: Am so.

REXX: Are not.

ISOBEL: I'm learning Italian.

REXX: You can name fashion designers and types of pasta.

NICKY: *(Breaking up the fight)* I like this movie. It's not as good as the first one or the third, but it has the kind of problems that are to be expected with the sequel to a major cultural phenomenon, but—

ISOBEL: I am so going to Italy. And you better watch it Buddy because I am going to make you sit here and watch nine hours of Federico Fellini once we get done with this thing.

REXX: Yeah? Want to fight about it? I can totally fight.

*(This is playful. REXX holds up his fists. ISOBEL retaliates with a pillow. He hits back. They laugh and pillow-fight. NICKY kind of stays out of it, trying to watch the movie, but maybe they get her—and, it's all good again—til—)*

*(NICKY's phone rings. It's home.)*

NICKY: Home.

ISOBEL: Don't answer.

*(NICKY doesn't.)*

*(Beat)*

*(Watching the movie)*

*(Thinking about Mom)*

*(Mom texts.)*

*(NICKY erases.)*

*(NICKY tries to tune out. She can't.)*

*(Finally NICKY plays the message on her V M.)*

*(We can hear slightly as she does the sound of a woman's voice—and she's hysterical. Exact words are hard to make out, like the sound of the grown-ups on The Peanuts specials. But the tone is clearly disturbing.)*

*(NICKY returns the call.)*

*(ISOBEL and REXX watch.)*

NICKY: Mom? Are you okay?
You left a message.
I know. Stop crying.
That's right.
Just take a breath. Are you breathing?
Yeah, I'll come over soon.
I don't know when.
Do you need me now?
Is he coming back?
Well, do you think he's coming back?
Mom, he'll come back. He lives there. He'll—
Well, you've kicked him out before and he came back before.
I know.
I'll be right there.
I know.
*(She looks at ISOBEL helplessly.)*

NICKY: I have to go back.

ISOBEL: Want us to come with?

NICKY: I have to go alone.

ISOBEL: You sure?

NICKY: The Death Star.

REXX: I'm sorry.

ISOBEL: If you make it The Death Star.

NICKY: No, it's really The Death Star.

REXX: My parents home is definitely The Death Star.
My dad's all Darth Vadar. My mom's—she just cries.

ISOBEL: You're both dramatic.

NICKY: Okay, my mom's getting hit and he left and she's hyperventilating. I think this is—

ISOBEL: Sure. I'm just saying. It's dramatic if you make it dramatic.

NICKY: I have to go.

ISOBEL: Sure.

NICKY: Do you—I mean, did I do something?

ISOBEL: Why do you think that ?

NICKY: I don't know...

ISOBEL: Don't be so insecure.

NICKY: Okay... Well. I'll be back in a few hours, I guess. I mean, is that okay? Can I come back?

ISOBEL: Of course you can come back.

NICKY: Okay. Well... May the force be with me.

(NICKY *puts her bag on and leaves.* REXX *gets his bag together.*)

REXX: I gotta go too.

ISOBEL: Okay. What are we doing later?

REXX: Um, I don't know. I may have plans...

ISOBEL: Oh. Okay.

REXX: Yeah. But I'll call you guys tomorrow.

ISOBEL: Sure.


## Alone Again, Or...

(ISOBEL *sits alone in the house. She's alone and it's finally quiet.*)

ISOBEL: *(To the air)* Hello, Mom? Hi there. Hi Mom... *(She picks up the phone. Dials. Leaves a message)* Hey,

Carla, it's me, Isobel. Your kid. Just leaving a message.
Everything's good here. Just touching base. Okay, well.
Hope you're having fun. Call me later and let me know
you're okay. Okay? *(She hangs up. Dials* NICKY's.*)* Hi.
It's Nicky's friend Isobel. I think she's on her way over.
Um, could you have her call me when she gets there?
Thanks. It's, um, important kind of. Thanks. *(Beat. She
dials one more number.)* It's me. Yeah, me Isobel. Are you
calling me and hanging up? Oh, really? Well, I think
it's you. No, that's lame. I don't have to forgive you,
Ever. You want to come over? Now. Bring ice cream.
Chocolate.

*(Meanwhile)*

*(*NICKY *takes a seat on the El train north.)*

*(*NICKY *sits, watching out the window.)*

NICKY: You can ride the El all the way to the end,
north, to the suburbs, further than Evanston, to the
Lake Street stop in Wilmette, and once you get there,
you can get a really expensive taxi-cab or you can call
your mom to pick you up. If your mom can drive. If
your mom is calm. If your mom can stand to get into
the car and focus on the road and stop screaming for
just long enough to, you know, come get you. And
sometimes, she can. Sometimes, she's even quiet. Not a
lot. But sometimes.

You don't hitchhike. You never hitchhike. You never
do anything really unsafe. Even if you think about it. It
would kill your mom. And someone is already doing
that.

## Letting Tiger In

TIGER: So, I'm here. Now what? You want to have sex?

ISOBEL: No.

TIGER: I miss you.

ISOBEL: Shut up.

TIGER: Okay.

ISOBEL: Why are you calling me and hanging up?

TIGER: Don't know what you mean.

ISOBEL: Come on. Don't play dumb.

TIGER: I'm totally over the whole thing. Our sordid past and all that.

ISOBEL: So why are you calling me and hanging up?

TIGER: You miss me too. You're acting all tough so your friends won't know. But I know. You miss me too.

ISOBEL: I don't miss you.

TIGER: Liar. I'm the only one who knows you.

ISOBEL: Whatever that means.

TIGER: It means I'm the only one who knows you. Want to go upstairs and have sex?

ISOBEL: No.

TIGER: So why'd you call?

ISOBEL: I thought we could talk.

TIGER: What do you want to talk about?

ISOBEL: I don't know. How's life?

TIGER: Amazing.

ISOBEL: You know, you really caused some damage.

TIGER: To your tender heart?

ISOBEL: To all of us. Before you left.

TIGER: Left?

ISOBEL: For rehab? Want to talk about that? Like how you stole money from my mother? How you hid out and didn't tell me your father was looking for you?

How you made me lie to cover your tracks, how you disappeared and ended up on the street—

TIGER: For like, a day or two. And it was totally safe and harmless.

ISOBEL: For you. Harmless for you because you knew that you'd get bailed out. Because we would have to bail you out. And it's all part of your game. How you love to test us, make people worry so you know we love you or something, and it's fucking lame and it has consequences, that game, like people get tired of playing it.

TIGER: Whoa.

ISOBEL: No you whoa. I mean, you just love making us worry and save you and shit. It's how you get us to prove we care.

TIGER: Slow down Sigmund Freud.

ISOBEL: We were really worried about you. I was. We didn't know where you were and then, when you finally surfaced, I mean, where you really were was worse than anything we'd even thought of—

TIGER: They were nice people.

ISOBEL: They were crackheads.

TIGER: But nice people. On crack.

ISOBEL: You put yourself in danger. And me too. You put me in danger. And you didn't even care.

TIGER: Look. That's all in the past. I went to rehab.

ISOBEL: Great. That fixes everything.

TIGER: You guys all need to look at yourselves, you know? It's so easy when the problem's me. But you have plenty of problems yourself and having me around makes it really convenient. But I'll tell you a couple of things about you Miss Razor's Edge, Miss I'm

So Free Because I'm Being Ignored and Neglected—
you have some pretty big—

ISOBEL: Fuck you.

TIGER: No. Fuck you.

ISOBEL: You don't know a thing about me. You never
did.

TIGER: Oh you'd be surprised what I know about you.
Why can't you be alone?

ISOBEL: I don't know what you mean.

TIGER: Why do you need someone around you all the
time? Like a mirror? Are you afraid you don't exist?
You take hostages. Nicky. And now that Rexx—

ISOBEL: Get out of my house.

TIGER: Gladly. But why are you afraid to be alone?
And what do you have to do to make sure that we'll all
stay and worship you all the time? Ever feel like a big
whore?

ISOBEL: I don't even know what you're talking about!

TIGER: You. And what lengths you will go to make
people love you. And do what you say. How you
change. In order to get this love. How you have
mastered the art of being on a pedestal. But I don't
think that's what you really want, is it? I think maybe
you want me to knock you off that pedestal. Want me
to knock you off the pedestal, Isobel?

(TIGER *moves towards* ISOBEL, *and she hits him. In the face.
Less than a punch, but more than a slap.*)

ISOBEL: Get out of my house!

TIGER: It's not your house. Like mother, like daughter.
You're just living off some dude.

(TIGER *leaves.* ISOBEL *slams the door after him. Hard*)

## Later That Night

(NICKY *returns. The roof [usually lit] is dark.*)

NICKY: Hey. Are you here?

(ISOBEL *turns on her flashlight. She's been sitting in the dark alone.*)

ISOBEL: You can't go home.

NICKY: I know.

ISOBEL: Don't go again.

NICKY: I'm right here.

ISOBEL: I need you to stay

NICKY: You do?

ISOBEL: Yeah.

NICKY: Like, you need me here?

ISOBEL: Yes, like I need you here.

(NICKY *takes this in.*)

ISOBEL: Just stay. Lets just—stay.

NICKY: Okay. I could just stay.

(*They lie down together. On the roof. Under the stars*)

ISOBEL: I'm sorry if I've been—

NICKY: It's okay.

ISOBEL: Lets just stay like this.

NICKY: Yes. Just like this.

ISOBEL: Lets not move. Ever.

NICKY: It's a deal.

ISOBEL: We'll just stay here.

NICKY: Sure.

ISOBEL: I'm scared.

NICKY: You're never scared.

ISOBEL: I know. But I am, kind of, now.

NICKY: What are you scared of?

ISOBEL: I don't know.

NICKY: You don't know?

ISOBEL: I don't know.

NICKY: It's okay. Everything's okay.

ISOBEL: Sure.


## The Summer Comes Undone

*(There is a distinct difference in* ISOBEL'*s demeanor from the last scene. Whereas we've just seen her vulnerable, here she is impenetrable.)*

*(*ISOBEL *puts a bunch of stuff in a garbage bag. Cleans out the room. Power cleaning)*

NICKY: What are you doing?

ISOBEL: Carla's coming home tomorrow.

NICKY: Oh.

ISOBEL: Gotta clean.

NICKY: Oh.

ISOBEL: *(Holding up the dress)* Want this?

NICKY: Yeah.

*(She seems very glum.* REXX *enters. He is bright and gleeful.)*

REXX: Yes. He's here. The man you've all been waiting for. Me. With Wings. Enter me with Wings.

*(*REXX *gets the camera. Starts filming* ISOBEL *and* NICKY *cleaning up and himself, narrating.)*

REXX: It was the last day of Summer. The girls cleaned up the roof. Threw away their trash. Packed it all in and said goodbye.

NICKY: Goodbye? *Not* goodbye.

ISOBEL: *(Still cleaning, to* REXX*)* You're in the way.

(NICKY *picks up the camera.)*

NICKY: We're not done. We haven't edited. We still have to edit.

ISOBEL: Too late.

NICKY: What do you mean too late?

ISOBEL: Summer's over.

NICKY: But—

ISOBEL: We move on.

NICKY: How?

ISOBEL: Let it go.

(NICKY *puts the camera down.)*

ISOBEL: *(Slightly softer)* Editing will come later. We'll put it on our list.

(ISOBEL *leaves to empty the trash.* REXX *follows.)*

(NICKY *crams her bag and pockets with whatever she can find—a sort of desperation for their objects overtakes her.)*

(ISOBEL *and* REXX *return with a new trash bag.)*

NICKY: What about the tapes? Who gets the tapes?

ISOBEL: I don't want them.

NICKY: I do.

REXX: I don't. I'll never watch them. Never. I live in "The Moment". I have no use for relics, artifacts, things that only live to remind us of things that ended….

NICKY: Well, I want them. I can't believe you guys don't.

ISOBEL: It's not that big a deal. I mean, we'll see each other.

NICKY: Of course we will!

ISOBEL: Let go. *(She continues cleaning.)*

*(NICKY takes the camera. She removes the cartridge.)*

*(ISOBEL leaves. NICKY puts the cartridge in her pocket.)*

*(We see NICKY in the present:)*

NICKY: The thing about footage is, it shows you a time that no longer exists. And you don't know who you'll be at each juncture, each time you watch it, the footage, the past. Only that you're someone else now. Looking back. Remembering. And let's hope you have some answers in the future, that you can give yourself in the past, making it all make sense. All this used to be analog. On tape. A thing you could keep. Now it's digital. It's just information. Digital information. Which you can store. In something called a Cloud. Where it can live. Forever if you want it to.)

*(She turns on the Play button and leaves the stage.)*

*(We see:)*

*(Footage)*

*(The following is video footage that we see—or possibly watch enacted—looped and repeating at the end as if to emphasize the moment that NICKY will replay indefinitely.)*

NICKY: …I think the problem's me.

ISOBEL: You how?

NICKY: Just me.

ISOBEL: I don't get that. How could the problem be you?

NICKY: I don't know. But it is. And, I mean, I don't want to blow the whole thing out of proportion or anything. Sometimes, maybe it just takes awhile to figure out where you belong.

ISOBEL: You belong here.

NICKY: Here how?

ISOBEL: With me. Want to stay?

NICKY: Stay how?

ISOBEL: For the summer. While Carla's gone. You could live with me, help me water the plants. Oh my God, we'll have so much fun. Say yes.

## END OF PLAY